Woman's

Illustrations by

Sandy Lynam Clough

Published by
The Paint Box Studio Press, Marietta, Georgia

Copyright © 1994 Artwork by Sandy Lynam Clough

Quotes from the Publisher's collection.

All rights reserved, including the right to reproduce this book or portions thereof in any form.

ISBN: 0-9613287-5-4

Published and printed in the United States by

The Paint Box Studio Press
*81 Whitlock Avenue
Marietta, GA 30064*

*(404) 499-7299
FAX (404) 427-5704*

10   9   8   7   6   5   4   3   2   1

Goodness is richer than greatness. It consists not in the outward things we do, but in the inward things we are.   E. H. Chapin

Life is an adventure in forgiveness.
Norman Cousins

Peace is not God's gift to His creatures. It is our gift to each other.
                                    Elie Wiesel

The future belongs to those who believe in the beauty of their dreams.
Eleanor Roosevelt

The first condition of lasting happiness is that a life should be full of purpose, aiming at something outside self.　　　　　　　　　　　　　　　　　　　　　　　　Hugo Black

Settle one difficulty and you keep hundreds away.
Chinese proverb

Wisdom is the reward you get for a lifetime of listening when you'd have preferred to talk.
Doug Larson

Reason deceives us often; conscience never.
Rousseau

The greatest use of life is to spend it for something that will outlast it.
William James

Children are like wet cement. Whatever falls on them makes an impression.
Haim Ginot

Sometimes the poorest man leaves his children the richest inheritance.
Ruth E. Renkel

Just remember in the winter, far beneath the bitter snow, lives the seed that, with the sun's love, in the spring becomes the rose.
 Warner Timberlane

Cooperation is doing with a smile what you have to do anyway.

It is a rough road that leads to the heights of greatness.
Seneca

Doing the tough things today will prepare us for the big things tomorrow.
Zig Ziglar

In time like these, it helps to recall that there have always been times like these.
Paul Harvey

Opportunity rarely looks like an opportunity. Often opportunity arrives incognito, disguised as misfortune, defeat, and rejection.
Dennis Waitley

Spirituality, unconditional love, and the ability to see that pain and problem are opportunities for growth and redirection---these things allow us to make the best of the time we have.
                                                                    Bernie Siegel, MD

Example is not the main thing in influencing others. It is the only thing.
                                        Albert Schweitzer

The secret to success in life is for woman to be ready for her opportunity when it comes.

I have found that if you love life, life will love you back.
Arthur Rubinstein

Find a need and fill it.
Ruth Stafford Peale

Anxiety is the great modern plague. But faith can cure it.
Smiley Blanton, MD

If you carry your childhood with you, you never become older.
                                    Abraham Sutzkever

No dream comes true until you wake up and go to work.
Banking

No one really knows enough to be a pessimist.
Norman Cousins

Be not afraid of going slowly, be afraid only of standing still.
Chinese Proverb

Happiness comes not from having much to live on, but having much to live for.
Tyrone Edwards

You can't turn back the clock, but you can wind it up again.
Bonnie Prudden

Comedy is simply a funny way of being serious.
Peter Ustinov

*It's not true that nice women finish last.
Nice women are winners before the game
ever starts.*

Goodness is something so simple: Always live for others, never seek one's own advantage.
                                                                    Dag Hammarskjold

Our prayers are answered not when we are given what we ask, but when we are challenged to be what we can be.
　　　　　　　　　　　　　　　　　　　　　　　　　　　　Morris Adler

A well-adjusted person is one who makes the same mistake twice without getting nervous.
Jane Heard

What counts is not necessarily the size of the dog in the fight---it's the size of the fight in the dog.
                                                                Dwight D. Eisenhower

Small deeds done are better than great deeds planned.
Peter Marshall

A great teacher never strives to explain her vision---she simply invites you to stand beside her and see for yourself.

An optimist is a woman who takes the cold water thrown on her idea, heats it with enthusiasm, makes steam and pushes ahead.   Anonymous

Joy is the feeling of grinning inside.
Dr. Melba Colgrove

There is no delight in owning anything unshared.
Seneca

It is believing in roses that one brings them to bloom.
French Proverb

There are people who have money and people who are rich.
                                                    Coco Chanel

Friendship consists in forgetting what one gives and remembering what one receives.
Alexandre Dumas the Younger

Blessed is the woman who can say that the girl she was would be proud of the woman she is.

Gratitude is the heart's memory.
French Proverb

Mistakes are the portals of discovery.
James Joyce

A baby is God's opinion that the world should go on.
　　　　　　　　　　　　　　　　　　Carl Sandburg

What really matters is what happens in us, not to us.
James W. Kennedy

There is one thing we can do better than anyone else: we can be ourselves.
William Arthur Ward

She who can suppress a moment's anger may prevent a day of sorrow.

Take time to be quiet.

The successful person is somebody who has integrity and is consistent.

People need loving the most when they deserve it the least.
Mary Crowley

The greatest single cause os a poor self-image is the absence of unconditional love.

God don't sponsor no flops.
Ethel Waters

People who talk to themselves are slightly above average in intelligence.
Joyce Brothers

When you cannot remove an object, plow around it---but keep plowing.

When you forgive somebody else you accept the responsibility for your own future.

I define love thus: The will to extend one's self for the purpose of nurturing one's own or another's spiritual growth.   M. Scott Peck, MD

Real love is when you do the things that are best for the person you love.

God's gift to you are your talents, your gift to God is what you do with those talents.

Worse than being blind would be to be able to see but not have any vision.
Helen Keller

You may give out, but never give up.
Mary Crowley

Children pay more attention to what you do than to what you say.
Mama Ziglar

By the time a woman realizes that her mother was usually right, she has a daughter that thinks she's usually wrong.

How many marriages would be better if the husband and the wife clearly understood that they're on the same side.

Man does not live by bread alone. From time to time he needs buttering up!

*Your children are not your children. They are sons and daughters of
Life's longing for itself...* Kahlil Gibran

I find that my life oscillates between being a morning person and an evening person. When I'm an evening person, I'm very creative, and when I'm a morning person I get a lot done.
                                                                    Nolan Bushnell

You can have everything in life you want if you'll just help enough people get what they want.
                                                                              Zig Ziglar

If your not failing occasionally, then you're not reaching out as far as you can.
Nolan Bushnell

Children make up a hundred percent of our future.

The most excited people on this earth are those who are growing.

Failure is the line of least persistence.

The only thing necessary for triumph of evil is for good men to do nothing.

People who have good relationships at home are more effective in the marketplace.

The picture you have of yourself is exactly the way you will perform.
Dr. Joyce Brothers

Outstanding people have one thing in common: an absolute sense of mission.

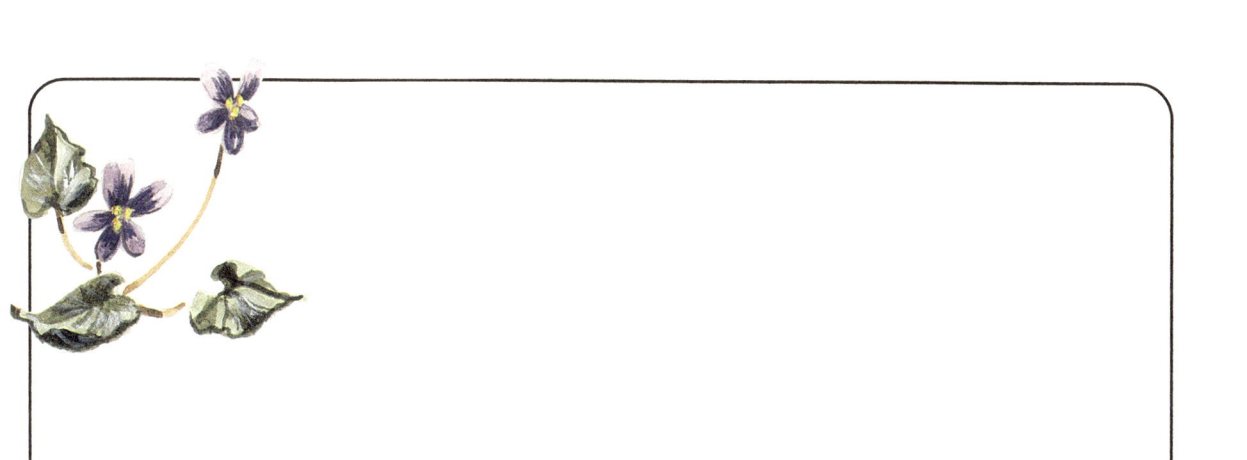

Work is the price we pay to travel the highway to success.

The only person who truly likes change is a wet baby.
Roy Blitzer

Worry is a misuse of the imagination.
Mary Crowley

We do not stop working and playing because we grow old. We grow old because we stop working and playing.

What lies behind you and what lies before you pales insignificant when compared to what lies within you.
                                                            Ralph Waldo Emerson

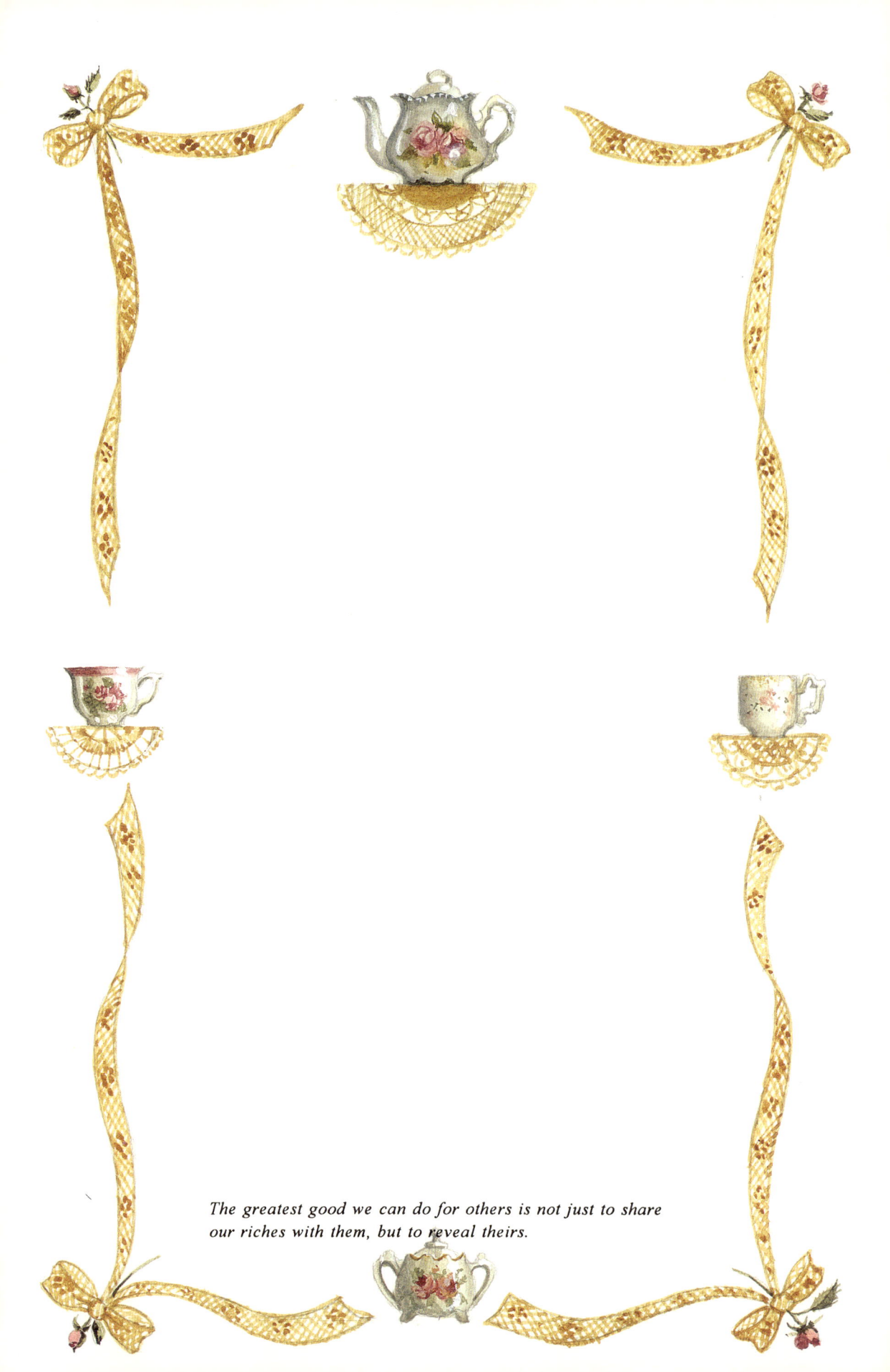

The greatest good we can do for others is not just to share our riches with them, but to reveal theirs.

No one is useless in this world who lightens the burden of it to anyone else.
Charles Dickens

*There've been 11 billion people to walk this earth,
but there's never been one like you.*

She has the right to criticize who has a heart to help.

Positive thinking will let you do everything better than negative thinking will.

*Children are not things to be molded,
but are people to be unfolded.*

Jess Lair

Enthusiasm is an inner fire that fuels the furnace od achievement.
William Arthur Ward

The best time to get started is when you have the idea.
Wally Amos

Adversity causes some women to break; others to break records.

Order Form for Paint Box Products

To order books with a name beautifully hand-lettered by a professional calligrapher, send that name and payment (check, money order, VISA or Master Card) to **The Paint Box Studio Press**. Please allow 4 weeks for delivery. (Canadian orders-US Dollars only.)

Woman's Journal, (record thoughts)..$14.95
Days of Glory, a Gentleman's Chronicle (planner) 14.95
Days of Glory, 14 notecards and envelopes 6.00
With Love From My Kitchen, Country Edition (for recipes).....................18.95
With Love From My Kitchen, Victorian Edition (for recipes)...................18.95
Roses in December (write life story) 14.95
Welcome to My Kitchen, (menu planner) 11.95
Recipe Cards (20 assorted) 3.00

Please send me:

_____
_____
_____

Name for cover (books only)

Cost of personalizing.................(please print)......$ 3.00
Shipping, one book.. 2.00
Shipping, each additional book....................... .50
Shipping, each package notecards...................1.00
Shipping, each package recipe cards................ .30
(*Georgia residents please add 5% sales tax*)

Address for mailing label:

_____
_____
_____

Charge card # MasterCard VISA   *Exp. date*

Signature

_____

Phone # (in case we have questions about your order, we need the number of the person placing this order)

_____

The Paint Box Studio Press
81 Whitlock Avenue
Marietta, GA 30064

(404)499-7299
FAX (404)427-5704